CLOUD-GLAZED MIRROR

CLOUD-GLAZED MIRROR
First Edition

Copyright © 2012 by Jim Bainbridge

Printed in the United States of America

Published in the United States by Elm Ridge Books,
an imprint of Silverthought Press
www.silverthought.com

Cover Artwork: "Mountain Lake Abstract Painting"
© 2011 by Phillip Jones

ISBN: 978-0-9841738-7-7

— ELM RIDGE BOOKS —
a Silverthought Press imprint

CLOUD-GLAZED MIRROR

—the poetry of—

JIM BAINBRIDGE

Acknowledgments

I am deeply grateful to Paulette Bates Alden and Sharon Doubiago, both of whom supplied encouragement and insightful comments along the way. And many thanks to Paul Evan Hughes for his sensitive, wise, and enthusiastic editing.

Thanks also to the editors of the following journals in which versions of these poems have appeared, sometimes with different titles:

And/Or: "Sudden Oak Death"
Arroyo Literary Review: "Blood" [nominated for a Pushcart Prize]
Atlanta Review: "Grandpa Remembers" [winner of an International Publication Prize]
Cold Mountain Review: "Before the Divorce"
Generations Literary Journal: "Not Much Time"
The Lindenwood Review: "A Winter Night in Amsterdam"
LIT: "Bookends of Grandpa's Marriage" [reprinted in *Caduceus*]
Palimpsest: "Wild with Spring"
Old Red Kimono: "Cloud-Glazed Mirror" [second place winner of the LaNelle Daniel Prize in Poetry]
Red Cedar Review: "The Abscission" [reprinted in *Yomimono* (Japan)]
Roanoke Review: "A Husk of Fog"
Santa Fe Literary Review: "My First Funeral"
REAL, Regarding Arts and Letters: "Meeting Her Parents"
SLANT, A Journal of Poetry: "Giving Her Back"
The South Carolina Review: "Wings without a Bird"
Third Wednesday: "Terminal" [co-winner of 2009 poetry contest]
Trajectory: "Stephanie's War"
Two Review: "Liminal Moments"
The Wisconsin Review: "Equipoise"

To my closest friend, Dan Fingarette,
whose contributions to this book have been invaluable.

Contents

I.

Before

Oh, to remember before memory
when the three of us
beginning mid-ecstasy
were for nine months a trinity,
their desire pulsing around me
as I lay quiescently submerged
in the dark, warm dream,
Dad probing that darkness,
thrusting himself over and over, faster
and faster toward me,
Mom's red iambic rhythm faster,
faster inside and all around me,
until his hands trembling in triumph
caressed, as if sculpting soft clay,
the ballooning belly where I floated,
comfortable, contented,
in the days before the wailing.

Equipoise

I

Grampy is resting on the old
wooden bench under our wisteria-covered pergola.

Blossoms hang in purple bunches from the rafters,
hiding us from the law.

Mom scolded us when she caught me
playing horsy on Grampy's shoulders again.

"I know. I know," he said. "But you should be kind
to an old man and a little boy doing what they love to
do."

So we galloped out here—"right on out
of the sheriff's jurisdiction," Grampy whispered.

He whinnied and jumped and rocked me side to side,
a bucking horse. Now, his head is drooped onto his
chest.

"Grampy, wake up." I tug on his hand. Slowly
he slides down against the back of the bench onto his
side.

Oh, he's just pretending to be asleep.
With my fingers, I push his lips, like soft clay,

into a pucker. They look funny
on his face, like blossoms.

I squeeze his nose—"Honk!"—and quickly pull
my hand away and jump back, expecting

he'll grab, then tickle me. But he stays
still. He's holding his breath. Isn't he?

II

I'm walking hand in hand with Dad—
past Mom's zinnias and chrysanthemums

and her roses blooming over a bed of white alyssum—
back out to the pergola. Dad sits me on his leg.
One of the pink roses has petals
splotched with yellow and brown,

and they've curled down their pouting lips.
Below them shadows of wisteria leaves sweep and flow.

III

A few days ago Dad shouted that Granny gave
some power she shouldn't have to an attorney.

Mom hugged me and said
Dad wouldn't be angry for long because

Granny just wants to be with Grampy.
He's been gone all summer.

Mom says Granny thinks not eating
will help her stop missing Grampy.

She says I should keep Granny company,
read to her, play games with her, ask her to eat with me.

Granny plays with me,
checkers and crossword puzzles,

and we listen to Mom's Bach cantatas.
But I've stopped asking her to eat with me.

Whenever I do, she says she's not hungry,
and then she cries and says she misses Grampy.

IV

I'm in her bedroom, watching her sleep.
The air is smelly—

her tea rose perfume, I guess—
and something else not so nice.

On the nightstand beside her bed
is the photo she says is Grampy

and her when they were married.
They don't look like Grampy and Granny,

but whenever I show it to her,
the picture makes her smile.

Shadows from her eyes,
nose, and creases in her cheeks rise

through long, thin rectangles of sunlight
streaming through the window.

She's holding her breath.
I try holding mine

for as long as she does,
but I can't.

Before the Separation

My hand inside Dad's
   I plop along barefoot
      in wet sand
         in the foamy highest
            reach of the waves.

Sheryl is talking with him
   about one of her college courses,
      but I'm listening to the screeching
         and whooshing sounds of the shore
            and smelling the salty, seaweedy scents.

I see a shell and pull
   away from his hand.
      It's a clamshell and beside it,
         a jagged piece of driftwood,
            like a withered old finger.

I pick up both and
   toss them back to the ocean.
      Dad and Sheryl laugh,
         and I turn and see
            them holding hands.

I run back and take his hand,
   the one she held. We begin
      walking again, my feet plopping

and stomping and kicking in the bubbly white
ribbons weaving their way along the shore.

Let's sit down here, Dad says.
 Can I go play in the waves?
  Okay, but only up to your ankles.
   I run to just past the foam,
    wait for the next wave,

and when it comes I catch
 some gritty water and throw
  a handful high in the air.
   I turn to see if Dad is watching.
    He and Sheryl are sitting close,

smiling at each other,
 and talking. Sheryl's hair
  so bright and blonde
   next to Dad's black, and their hands
    are together again, Dad's on top of hers.

I turn back toward
 the waves, run out farther,
  chasing the receding water.
   A wave crashes into me
    and knocks me over.

Salty water rushes
 into my mouth and nose.
  Sand scrapes my back and legs.
   I struggle, choking. *Dad! Dad!*
    A hand grabs my arm

and pulls me up.
    Dad's face looks
        scared, angry.
           Can't I even hold—
           I start crying.

Dad pulls me along,
    back to dry sand.
        He lets go of my arm,
           takes a couple of steps
               away from me and stops.

He looks at Sheryl,
    shakes his head slowly,
        turns back toward me,
           kneels in the sand, opens his arms—
           My son—and the whole
        world tilts toward
    those strong,
warm arms.

Not Much Time

This morning, on the train
in that cherry-blossom-brief
world between wakefulness and sleep
I opened my eyes while sitting
on Dad's lap
saw buildings, trees, cars, bridges
smeared across a rain-veined
image of him, arms around me.

My remembrances of him,
are like that now,
flying by in an Impressionist blur,
as if painted by one who knows
there's not much time.

Not much time to snuggle
closer,
close my eyes,
feel his breathing,
the beating of his heart,
the vibrations of his deep voice,
the clicking and the rocking.

A Husk of Fog

When I was a child, I
repeatedly asked my
father, What am I?
He seldom led me
to the same answer twice:
the boy he loved with all his heart,
a story I told myself,
the working out of a kiss
planted years before,
evolving strategies for dealing with the world.

One day, while meditating with
me cross-legged on the floor of his study,
he suggested that I become
fully attentive to myself and
answer my own question.

I found a heart beating, the quiet
rise and fallback of breath, the pressure
of my body touching the floor—
and silence
drifting into my mind,
like fog spills over hills
and down into valleys,
seeking its shape in emptiness.

Wild with Spring

I ran through fields of
clover and wild mustard
with Lily, our white German shepherd,
running ahead and back.
When I fell to the ground,
panting, laughing, the sky
swirled with cirrus clouds
like blueberries and cream.

Lily was wild with spring
eager to move on, to swim,
in the feral ocean
of fumes oozing from the ground.
She ran in circles around me,
licked my face, leaned back, barking,
her front legs set,
ready to leap.
A frightened rabbit ran.

Heaving for breath, I found Lily
lying on her stomach, holding
the rabbit in her paws,
pulling and tearing
sinewy flesh with her teeth.
I touched her side. She growled
as she turned her head toward me.
Her tongue dripped

reddish saliva, and white
fur clung to her nose
and the edges of her jaws.

I lay on my stomach and pressed
my face to her side.
The stink of rabbit innards
seeped through her fur.
My chest grew hollow
and darkness passed over me
as if I'd been grazed
by a black feather.

Licking my face, Lily fetched me
back to consciousness.
Spots of blood and wisps of fur
soiled a bowl of crushed clover.
I started back home. Lily
romped in the mustard along the way.

Blood

Against an out-of-focus
background consisting of
a section of the yard wall
smothered under English ivy—
a favored habitat of spiders,
ants, beetles, and many other
little creatures delightful
to my boyish curiosity—
Lily, our white
German shepherd, stands
in front of my older brother, Jace,
near a tuft of lavender-pink
autumn crocuses poking
out of the lush, green lawn.

Lily's head, near the left
side of the photo, is turned
toward the camera; her ears
point slightly back,
wary of Jace's antics;
her tongue suspends
a drop of saliva from its tip;
her body extends across
the photograph, in the far right
side of which her tail bends mid-wag,
having just been pulled
by Jace, whose guilty

left hand and arm hang limp,
pretending innocence,
across her age-thickened back.

He kneels, almost hidden
on the far side of her;
his head tilts down slightly;
his chin, half-buried in
her bristly white coat, rests
on her back; and behind
a frond of straight, blond hair
dangling nearly to his lips,
his squinting sky-blue eyes,
his mischievously furrowing brow,
and his puckering lips
present an expression he used
to tease Lily and me. More than once
I wished she would
nip him, draw just a little blood.

Giving Her Back

How different we were—I
having known rabbits and birds with
my eyes, ears, language, and culture;
she with her eyes, ears, nose and teeth.
And in what different worlds we lived—she
wholly in the present, brimming and bright,
her happy bark and eager tail often waking me
from daydreams in which I imagined
the future, the past, or other abstractions
that bestow no scent.

Early on she chose the shady place
between two plum trees—
right in the middle of a bed of Mom's prized flowers—
for napping on hot afternoons.

Annually, Mom's irritation bloomed.

I once witnessed the two of them face off.
Lily! You hairy nuisance.
Get out of there!

Lily regally lifted
her head off the cool ground littered
with newly flattened flowers, opened
her jaws, let out her huge tongue,
and, though she averted her

eyes from Mom's glowering stare,
made a face that expressed,
Fuss all you want, lady,
but this spot belongs to me.

Mom said it would be all right
to bury Lily in that favored spot.

Over the hole he'd dug,
Dad quoted Epictetus:
Never say of anything
that I have lost it,
only that I have given it back.

Beside Lily's body
at the bottom of the grave,
I placed her dinner
and water bowls, Frisbee,
tennis ball, leash,
and three old shirts of mine
she'd collected in her house.

Good-bye, Lily, I said,
knowing she wouldn't be
there to lie on and crush
the flowers that, come summer,
would blossom on her grave.

My First Funeral

Dad lifted the terra-cotta lid
to show me silvery white ashes,
shards of discolored bone—
nothing there that resembled Uncle—
then placed the urn in a hole
in the garden verge.

We who live—he began to say,
but Mom cut him off: *I don't want any words.*
Dad shoveled loose dirt over the urn,
and placed a dark gray stone on top.
Words were chiseled in the stone,
but I couldn't read them.

Glancing behind us, I saw
the sun about to dip
below hills, and I remembered
Uncle once telling me
that night doesn't fall
from the sky like
a hangman's hood.
It's day that descends, gliding,
enraptured by bird song,
down from the eastern sky.

Night rises
like mist from low-lying

pools of shadow and flows
out from hills and trees,
quietly ascending
as it snuffs out light.

The Lake

I

Side by side, facing the inverted sky,
Dad and I sat on this granite boulder.
Ceremonies of solitude he called
these times together
amid the water-world drama of
trees and clouds and
shoreline's blue-green weave of light—
so unlike the dramas at home.

We seldom spoke
while sitting here,
though this final time,
in the summer before I entered
high school, after doctors found
his terminal cancer,
he said, "Your mother and I
sometimes say things
to each other that we don't really mean.
You know that, right?"

I simply nodded. He put
his arm around my shoulder
and pulled me closer. "Life is
a process of finding things we love
and then losing them."

I nodded again,
the only sounds: wind
in the trees, chirring
of insects, bird calls,
waves whispering, Shhh, shhh,...
like a father, *Pa-shhh-ence, pa-shhh-ence.*
Everything will be all right, or,
I imagined, like the hospice nurse
who visited us the night before
might on some future day whisper,
Pa-shhh-ence, pa-shhh-ence.
This won't take all that long.

II

His cremains were portioned in thirds—
to Mom, my brother, and me.
I brought my share here, sat
for a while amid gauzy patterns of gnats,
remembering him and
our ceremonies of solitude,
then opened the lid of the clay jar.
Milk-gray ashes resembled the sky.
Some sank in the water, some
floated, spreading out, drifting
toward the other shore
on a breeze that parted us
as we'd lived, quietly, Dad and I,
going our separate ways
into the unknown
future that swallows every
good-bye.

Liminal Moments

Pokes and jabs of blades
of grass and clumps of dirt
make her bare feet feel free as
she walks between rows of her family's vineyard vines.

The warm sunlight reminds her of how
her skin awoke as it pressed for the first time
against my skin; of how, since then,
her clothes feel good in a new way when she puts them
on; and of how the spray of warm water in a shower
now gives her goose bumps of delight.

She knew the vines would have grown
heavier in her absence, but now
they're exquisitely filled out, the soil
around them soft and comforting,
the air redolent of green.

She runs her fingers from the ground
up along a trunk, caressing
its jagged calluses. She kisses
a leaf, feeling with her lips
its velvety underside,
licks a small cluster of
green orbs of nascent fruit

and remembers saying

You sure seem to have an erection a lot of the time

remembers

> my glancing down at it
> and turning my profile to her,
> torso arching back slightly to form
> a v-shape with my erection

remembers my reply

> *It's the way my body smiles at you.*

She wraps her arms and legs around the vine,
looks up at the cirrus-feathered sky,
feels sunshine pour
through leaves onto her back,
and pinches dirt between her toes—
as her body shivers
its own shimmering smile.

Meeting Her Parents

As the huge wrought iron gate parted,
each half turning inward
on a massive stone pillar,
I saw for the first time
the broad expanse leading
to her parents' villa:

green blaze of lawn,
oak and walnut trees,
Japanese maples modeling
their crimson and bronze late-summer dresses,
ornamental grasses, tree ferns, and a profusion
of flowers, their colorful sex
organs perfuming the air
with multi-layered fragrances of desire,

all canopied with clouds and sky—
white, gray; white, gray, blue; white, gray—
over tawny California hills that,
she said, pointing,
would be carpeted
with wildflowers in May,
when we would marry in May,
lupines, coreopsis, golden poppies
and salvia, their blossoms waving—
she turned to me and smiled—
waving, purple and erect in the warm spring air.

Joy of Having a Girl

daffodils in bloom
the baby
finds her toes

crevices in
the folds of her baby skin—
scent of yogurt

she asks how far
one Mississippi, two…
too soon she'll leave home

she wrestles with boys
enjoy them, I think, enjoy
your breastless days

she asks
why are we here
star-glutted sky

her bookcase
empty space of two volumes—
in college now

II.

Bookends of Grandpa's Marriage

I

Our budget tight, we rented
a two-person kayak and
honeymooned on the Russian River—
otters playing, ospreys mounting the air with silver
flesh wriggling in their talons, towering
redwoods exuding their resinous perfumes,
harbor seals basking in the sun,
and, rising from the ocean near river's end,
huge, craggy-edged sea stacks around which
waves splashed and swirled, pounded and roiled,
as gulls, like sleek white kites, dived
and soared in the salty air.

Surrounding vineyards were draped
in sunlit autumn colors when
we put in upstream, then found
a place to camp on
a secluded patch
of the river's shore.
You prepared our meal.
I set up our home: tent,
sleeping bag, air mattress, thermal unit.
The air was cool and clear. The river
chuckled softly. Our cups and plates

were made of plain white paper,
but the sky was Wedgwood blue.

We snuggled in our sleeping bag and gazed
out of the tent flap at a clear night sky.
The stars seemed more numerous
and closer than ever before, as though
the two of us had been elevated
into the heavens.

Morning. Light fog muted
the previous day's vibrancy,
but the misty view
was romantic, and several times
we pulled the kayak onto the shore
to walk the hills and make
love in the musty leaves.

We arrived at river's end in time
to watch the sun puff itself up
and slide, liquefying, into the sea.
A flocculent canopy of pastels
floated in vaporous milky blue.
You sighed, having wanted
a wild vermillion sunset to stun
the ocean, the sky,
and me.

But I like pastels, I said.
My favorite picture is full of pastels.

What picture is that?

I framed your face with my fingers.
Pale blue eyes, light blonde hair,
cheeks flushed from exercise.

How's this for pastel? you said,
and stuck your tongue through the frame.

How's this for wild? I answered—
and when we next
looked up, the stars
were glittering again.

II

Now, the low December sun descends,
     mullioning the yard with
shadows of naked trees.
     Chilly breezes picked their leaves
that feathered out in spring
     and raked them into the lee of things.
And you're not here.

I'm sitting under the pergola
     petting Taffy, her soft
coat, her thickening flank.
     She's getting old, too.
I've already taken her
     for her afternoon walk.
Archipelagoes of little yellow locust leaves

were steeping in shallow puddles
on the shoulders of the drive.
    As you know, she dislikes
getting wet and trod
    carefully around the puddles
with her large white paws.
    The world suddenly appeared
aqueous. You
    weren't there.

A gust of wind worries
    the dormant vines above us.
They clatter like the wings of
    startled birds, reminding me that
you are not
    here.

By darkening degrees
    sallow dusk settles in.
Oh, my love,
    your pillow
has lost the scent
    of your hair.

Grandpa Remembers

Remember the dawn: leaves
unfurling, moist, glowing with
their green future, suckling
the sun, dappling light over
yellow tree-sperm snaking across the drive.

Remember midday shadows contracting,
wildflowers on hills that hung
from a lake-blue sky,
the ripening smell of sun on our skin
like rain on warm flagstone.

Remember the afternoon, lying together, dreaming:
a beach home, grandchildren building sandcastles.
Vultures soared on rising pillars of air,
their noses searching,
while on the horizon dusk whistled
as it dug our graves.

Terminal

Window: scrim of ice.
Soiled drifts of sodden snow.
Skeletal tree.
Naked branches claw the weary sky.
Black hunger caws,
stabbing brittle air,
hunger, blood, hunger.

Like a final sigh
dusk settles into darkness.
Sullen silence spreads.
Spectral tree.
X-ray shadow
of a suffering sky.
Black hunger stabs again.

The tumor spreads.
Sullen, gray.
Arsenal of more
colonizing shadows,
stabbing silent
foreshadows of
the broad black wings.

Cloud-Glazed Mirror

Faintly sexual scent of
the shore, a gull's cry,
dragonflies hovering like indecisions.
In a few months, the rains
will come in earnest,
and the winter mist she loved
to watch rise in tendrils
occluding the far-shore hills,
today faint furrows of misty gray.

Do her ashes still
mingle in these waters?
Algae-bearded stones,
minnows darting away,
fallen leaves sliding
over the water's wrinkled skin
like an old lover's fingers.

If this cloud-glazed mirror could
think, not just reflect,
would it think
my face is just another
passing whitish evanescent thing?
Not long ago a boy's. With her.
I reach down.
It trembles.

Frank's Otherwise Ordinary Morning

I jerk awake

gasping

for breath

I'm in the wrong body

in a strange bedroom

neither in the present

nor the past

but in that feral

world

between was and is

grayish light

leaks

in around

the edges of

curtains

I listen carefully

nothing

my right hand   tingles

feels

numb

I'm having a stroke

                              I take my pulse

                    faster
                                        than normal
              much faster

I shake my tingling hand
                              is it getting worse

        get up
                    get going
                                    don't get
              all wound up
                                    panicky
                    again
                                        over
nothing

        the carpeted bedroom
                          floor feels
              unsteady
                              as if
                        about to buckle
                                    or give way
if I fell through   I'd get
                                    impaled
on something
                          a spear of broken two-by-four
              nobody would find me for days

stepping quickly
                    onto the bathroom tiles
        my feet feel
                    bloated
                    cushioned with water

I put one foot   up
                    on the side
                    of the tub
                        and examine it   toes
                                              arch
                                              soles
        nothing unusual
            that I can see
                            fingers feel bloated too
        there must be
                    something   seriously   wrong
that I can't see
                    or maybe I really did
                    wake up in the wrong body

stop this nonsense
                    how could you wake up in the wrong body

shave   shower   go down   make a strong cup of coffee
eat breakfast
                    everything will be fine
                                    you'll get in your car
                                    drive to the office
        and everything will be fine

walking
      down
         the stairs
      my feet still waterlogged
    the light in the kitchen
                is unnatural   bluish
misty
        as if a cloud settled in overnight
    and everything   the appliances
           the dishes
           the coffee and cereal
               set out for breakfast
      all give the impression
           of turning away
               of hiding
from something
        have things been moved around

    something   someone
      is in this house   with me
           my arms and legs break
    out in gooseflesh
      if only I had   a dog
        it would be growling at
        the unseen
and at   this unnatural quiet
     no appliances purr
       nothing moves
    a stillness I could evaporate into
only the wall clock ticks   unusually loud
    with a hollow muted echo
        I've never heard before

above closed blinds
        through the kitchen's
     round clerestory window
                    the trees aren't moving
        they're whispering
            don't be fooled
               by all this green
            don't be fooled

       and on the neighbor's russet-tiled roof
where
              are the pigeons
    that pace back and forth
          where are the other birds
      I don't hear their morning songs

have they sensed it too   this wrongness
       and scattered like shadows
          into the imagined
       safety of bushes

the air suddenly trembles   outside   on the other
side
       of the house
   children screech
          probably on their way to school
      they don't see it
         the sky
         the birds hiding

each time I blink

            the world goes
      dark

    the lids must be staying shut too long
                  there must be something
        wrong in my brain

            I am having a stroke
         I'm afraid to blink again

   if I do
          will the lids reopen
         will I ever see again

  the clock's ticking
        I know why it's so loud   with that eerie
echo

  it has to work
        harder
           to keep going
     because the whole world is congealing
             might at any moment set
     everything trapped
            as in amber
   everything   forever   still

above

      the neighbor's

            russet tiles

                is a room full of sky

    white gray   white gray blue   white gray

that relentless one word of the clock is driving me crazy

I reach for   the coffee cup   lying

      upside down

          in the drying rack

    my hand hurries

         to stay inside the hand

              I see reaching for the cup

      its fingers

         bend without breaking

            and touch the cup

                  cool

                  hard

                  round

        familiar yet strange

      the cup is still there

I hear   echoes
             remnants
                  of voices spoken
                            laughed
                            cried
      here   in this very room

   I turn and turn
          and shudder
                  as the voices
                        disappear
                        the clock even louder
now
           tick!   tick!

  the sky is pressing down
                it's going to frighten
     all the birds
         they'll explode
                out of the bushes
                    crash into the windows
    I'll be hit by flying glass
                I'll be blinded by shards
            one in each eye
     my jugular vein will be severed

        I'm dying

you should know

               by now

                   whenever you start

                         trembling like this

            think of something else
                okay
                    okay

first primes
      2 3 5 7 11 13 17 19 23 29 31 37 41
                           is 41 prime

                  something is
           terribly wrong

                    a blood clot
     in the left
              side of my brain

           this is the refrigerator
           this is the table
           $\Pi = 3.14159$
           the square root of 169 is 13

the sky has suddenly taken on
a pallid timbre like its death
sigh between dusk and darkness
I can feel it pressing
pressing down
that's why the trees aren't moving
that's why there aren't any birds

my heart is pounding
it's going to explode
this is the sink
this is the faucet
Freud's address was Berggasse 19, Vienna

tick!   tick!
this is the stove   the coffee pot   the jar of instant
this is not my hand
not my body
not my kitchen
not the echoes of my voice
not my silence
portending
not pause but stop

how did I get here
can't breathe   can't get enough air
how do I get out

tick!
tick!
tick!
tick!

43

Like a Breeze on Its Way to Someplace Else

He waves. The taxi
pulls away from the curb.
For a moment, light
gleams off tears on her face.
His hand goes back and forth,
back and forth, near the rear window,
as if washing. Or erasing.

She takes a step forward.
"Bye, honey! I love you. Be careful."
He doesn't say anything, just
lets the taxi continue,
sees her run
a few steps toward him,
stop, wave frantically,
open her mouth. He can't hear

what. She's getting smaller now,
lets her arms fall,
this woman he'd lived with
for eighteen years. Smaller.
She bends over, puts her hands
on her knees, faces down
toward the sidewalk, her body heaving
up and down. He keeps waving,
even though she can't

see. With each wave,
she's getting smaller.

Special Soap

I

On her way back to Grandma Tran's room
at the tea plantation's guesthouse,
a man grabbed Amy and pressed
a cloth to her face. She tried to scream
but couldn't, the sweet smell,
nauseating, pulling her close…

She lay on damp grassy ground,
woozy and hurting in places.
Insects hummed, and stars
and a nearly full moon floated above.
Headlights drew close.
A car stopped beside her.
Uncle Phuong rushed out
and scooped Amy up in his arms.

II

Amy repeatedly washed her hands and face
in a yellow-stained bathroom sink.
Something was on them, Amy was certain,
something she couldn't point to, couldn't see.

"Would you like me to give you a bath?" Grandma asked.
"Uncle went to our village to get a very special soap."

"What's special about it?"

"Everyone says it cleans like nothing else can."

Singing songs Amy had never heard before,
Grandma washed Amy everywhere
with the jasmine-scented soap, even in places
only her mother back in San Francisco
had ever washed her, places that now ached.

"Ow," Amy said, just once.

"Sometimes, honey, if we get really dirty,
it hurts a little to get completely clean."

"Why did that man grab me?"

"He wanted a little money. That's all.
And now you're completely clean,
and you can go back to being a happy, carefree little girl."

III

Grandma and Amy walked outside hand in hand
into warm air redolent of green
and joined Uncle under a large tree limb.
He lifted Amy onto a swing.
Her hands held tightly
on to the rough hemp ropes.

She moved out and up
into broad, deep daylight.
Row upon row of tea bushes flowed into the distance,
matting with mossy green the serrated horizon of hills,
above which clouds curved in waves,
like a giant fingerprint in the sky.

Down over contoured rows of leaves.
Down over moist earth that exuded the sweaty odor of
field labor.
Back and up into Grandma's hands.
Then down again, picking up speed,
out and up, the wind in her face,
and just as she began to slow down,
an urge arose, prompting her to let go—
let go now, you're free to go—
but Amy held more tightly
on to the tethering ropes.

Down, down again,
and back up
into Grandma's hands. "Would you like
to go a little higher?"

"Yes, please—
but don't go away."

Stephanie's War

Juan and I sit hand in hand beneath
the old valley oak tree in Mom
and Dad's backyard. A crow caws
on a distant branch. The gleaming black
hunger spreads its wings and oars
into the air, its sharp eyes searching for death.

A storm is coming—roiling clouds, wind
portending rain. A murmuration of
starlings enshrouds the twilight sky. I look
down and see Lady, her white fur streaked with
blood, lying beside a dark hole, dark like
the unmoving shadow of something unseen.
Of course! It was Lady who died.
How could I have thought it was Juan?

The starlings screech, swarming
above me in the tree. Suddenly,
it's dark and I'm in Mom's garden,
my feet mired in a thick suck of mud.
"Where's Juan?"

Mom cuts one of her white roses and
places it on a towel-wrapped package.
"Juan should be home soon. These are
his favorite cinnamon rolls, nice and fresh
and warm. Take them out to him."

I'm walking along a dark street,
carrying the fragrant package
against my chest. The warmth
from the rolls rapidly dissipates.
Juan drives up in his Camaro, opens
the door. "Why are you crying?"

"Your rolls have gone cold."

He reaches for a strawberry,
wet and red like a wound,
pushes it through rounded lips.
I open the towel, and a snake covered with blood
leaps out and bites into my arm.

My eyes open with a start. The skeletal
gray arms of the oak tree rise
crookedly and pleadingly into
the leaden sky. Juan's face is buried
in my lap. One of his hands lies open,
fingers relaxed, slightly curled,
as if having let everything gathered fall away.
He sits up, eyes closed,
face distorted, ashen—

I wake in my childhood bedroom.
A crow is perched on the edge of my dresser.
I try to scream for Mom and Dad, but
I've lost my voice. The crow glares
at me with its black-currant eyes, then shimmies
its tail and poops. Mom will be upset. I take off

my pajama top and start mopping up
the mess. I look around my room,
trying to figure out how I can hide this
from Mom, but over my shoulder she says
that from now on Lady will have to stay
outside in her own house.

I turn and look out the window to
where Juan's car should be and see
waves roiling and foaming on a shore.

Suddenly, he's here, peeling
back our flowered quilt,
smiling down at me.
He's so beautiful and full of detail
that I know with certainty
I've finally awakened and he's alive:
black hair tumbling over eyes
glimmering their moist desires,
full ripe lips hinting at some imminent surprise,
dark nipples taut in arousal,
shallow pool of his navel,
twin furrows forming a V along
the sides of his abdomen, drawing
my eyes down, down.

"I have something to show you," he whispers,
pointing at his chest. Growing
on it are three poppies, their red
blossoms open wide, as if
smiling at a warm summer sun.

"That's amazing! They're beautiful.
Where did they come from?"

"I was walking,
on patrol."

"You're alive!" I say as he lowers
himself onto me. "I was only dreaming!"

I cry holding him, cry feeling
his arms around me, his warmth
flowing into me, his soft hair brushing
my throat. "You're alive!
It's so amazingly wonderful that you're alive!"

"Of course I'm alive. Are you still having
those nightmares about snipers in Kandahar?"

"Yes," I say, as the poppies bleed
syrupy red nectar onto his chest.

Change

The photograph is
static, she said,
yet it flows,
as if strangely alive.
Dad stands behind Mom,
she behind me,
my head a restless leaf
with eyes, concealing
her pubic hair.

Smile lines that
never will mature
carve glyphs of radiance
round Dad's mouth.
He appears,
with naked wife
and daughter before him, pleased;

but every time I try to penetrate
with memory the distance of
so many years,
Mom's face and my face
seem to have changed.
My eyes sometimes
squint, sometimes smile,

sometimes signal
curiosity, sometimes try
to see a future me
peering back at a pale-moon
face, and beside it crescents,
one waxing, one waning,
of the larger planet
of Mom's hips.

She appears thoughtful,
sometimes showing irritation
with her brilliant husband
and frisky child,
sometimes pondering
one of the engineering problems
he shared with her, sometimes

concerned that he still
hasn't repaired the roof
or that he doesn't spend
enough time with me, or her,
though he already had
changed as much as he ever would.

The Abscission

A retired professor of Japanese
literature, a formerly austere
and powerful man who had taught
that haiku are the stepping
stones of a path to satori,
suffers a paralytic stroke
leaving him unable
to communicate other than by
moving his eyes. His vital
organs begin to fail. Doctors give
him only a week or so to live.
He indicates that he wants
his sixteen-year-old grandson
to take him home to Kyōto,
where cherry trees are
beginning to bloom.

The boy cares for his grandfather—
bathes him, reads to him from *The Tale of Genji*,
cleans the soiled sheets and clothes—
and is repeatedly awed
while massaging his elder's arms and legs
by how soft they are, how yielding.
He had loved his grandfather before,
but the major component of that love
had been respect. Now, the boy feels
a pang of tenderness

and warmth, springing from
the fragility and evanescence of
his grandfather's life.

One crystal-blue-sky afternoon,
while the grandfather and boy sit
together in the garden,
the boy holding his grandfather's hand,
clouds gather over nearby mountains;
and as they do, the boy senses,
as though from the paralyzed hand,
that his grandfather wants to write
a death poem. The boy asks whether this is so.
His grandfather's eyes move to the right—yes.

Just then the boy sees a sun-
stunned cherry blossom fall.
He looks up again at
the transforming sky and is surprised
to hear himself say:

>Rain clouds overhead
>a deep, black silence—a flash
>we live and are gone.

"Was that your death poem, Grandfather?"
Eyes move to the left—no.

Again, the boy looks at the cherry tree,
sees in it pink, white, gray,
its leaves fluttering, nuzzled by a gentle breeze;
and feeling a tingling from

his grandfather's hand, he whispers:

> To life's eastering
> shadow, how great the speed of
> color through the trees.

"Was that your death poem, Grandfather?"
Eyelids slowly lift. No.

Now, the boy looks carefully
at the cold, bony, withered hand,
seeing exquisite beauty, perfect
like a blossom on a tree, so fleeting.
The next moment he feels
he is in his grandfather's body,
unable to move or talk.

Looking out from those tired old eyes,
he experiences neither fear
nor anxiety. What he sees is
his young self sitting close by,
blooming with youth, holding
a wizened hand in a young hand,
and he thinks during an exhale
that seems never to end:

> Exuberant spring—
> so soon crow's feet at your eyes
> and withered desires.

Returned suddenly to his accustomed self,
the boy notices another

cherry blossom quiver, let go,
and asks, "Was that
your death poem, Grandfather?"—
but the eyes do not move.

A Winter Night in Amsterdam

It had been a long walk
back from the party, the canals
dark under the fogged-in,
spectral city lights; the slap, slap,
lick, lick of waves against the hulls of boats;
the eerie lowing of foghorns in the distance.

I brushed snow out of my hair and reached
for the handle of the gate leading
to my apartment complex. I felt
suddenly exhausted by the raw,
icy metal in my bare hand, by the
blade-cold air with its gray clouds
of breath, by the cold in my face that hurt,
the cold in the snow-covered streets.

I pushed on the gate—its metallic squeak.
Birds burst out of white hedges.
One lay near my feet. A sparrow.
So quiet. The silence that arrives and stays.
Flowers nearby were black.

Snow had piled up around
the base of an old linden tree,
and bunched like pillows
in the tree's crotches, and stretched
out like dunes of white sand

along the tops of its branches;
and under the weight of snow and ice,
the old tree creaked wearily in the cold.

Earlier, near sundown, I had noticed through mist
five crows perched high in the tree's
skeletal gray branches. I wondered
whether the crows were still up there, sleeping
under pelts of snow. If they were, at daybreak
they would breakfast on sparrow.

Wings without a Bird

The imagined ambassadors
    we optimistically send across
        the boundaries that separate us,

words—in reality nothing
    more than components of instructions
        to guide the listener's or reader's imagination—

expose only themselves
    and point, as the fingers
        of spectators point toward

but cannot give the experience
    of the blossoming of the event
        so many have come to see.

We are beings who can
    feel but cannot be felt,
        and who, desperate

to overcome
    this experiential disconnection,
        desire love, literature, music

and all other forms of art—
    and the eternity
        it would take to succeed.

Sudden Oak Death

when the wind blows
                    as now
i whisper
          my chorus of leaves
the long memory
              that rings through me

centuries ago
            gray squirrel
buried me
          forgot to retrieve me
shocked
         by a flash of moisture
i swelled
         tunneled down
into rich earth
          the graveyard
all land is
       and rose
dreaming of light
              air
rain
      dragonflies
birds singing
        rose
in slow

heliotropic

lust

        and pollen-love

ejaculated

        by nearby trees

on seminal gusts

        of wind

flash of days

        blink of nights

so many years

        and then

from beyond

        where the sweet

blue-gray air

        alloys with

distant hills

        they came—

the sun

        keeping its distance

and the moon—

        humans

their hair-

        deficient skins

covered with skins

        and hair of others

their hot blood

        unlike the slow

dulcet rise

        of our sap

raced and roiled

                              how the male
went at the female
                              what frenzy

lacking our rootedness
                                        they made of us
wagons
                    ships
houses
                    fences
cradles
                    coffins
wine barrels
                              ink for writing
tannins for tanning
                                        charcoal that fired
the augural roar
                              of their iron weapons
and machines
                              that cut and dig
uproot and blast
                              and fly
and spew into the air
                                        poisons
that send quivers
                              through our leaves

and the birds
                    for so long
so many
                    in the green

harbor
                of our limbs
the breathy flutter of
                        their wings
their welter of
                fruity whistling
at the bluing
                of dawn
disappearing
                        leaving behind
silence
                and insects
that devour
                our blossoms
leaves
        and bark

summers are hotter
                drier now
cankers in my bark
                bleed black sap
brown spots spread
                in my leaves
and when the wind blows
                        as now
i whisper
                adumbrations
of death-
                enriched earth

Autumn

Time of bright skies and chilly breezes,
of fairs and harvests and Halloween,
when downy cloudlets snail
over tawny hills, and faster,
faster the clock of trees,
deceptive hands of leaves
becoming gorgeous
     as they die,

   when russet echoes
   the green command of spring
   and volant hunger descends to glean
   withered fields and cider-
   scented orchards of over-ripe fruit,

when plaintive evensongs
of crickets wind down
and grasshoppers drag
themselves along and torpid
flies struggle clumsily
against night's frosty call.

   Brimful world—so much to lose.
   The lushness of spring and summer falls
   under the shadow of winter coming on,
   and lives once full of love
   wither to an endurance of longing.

Maine Fishing Harbor

susurrus of the shore
chords of bird hunger
low of fog horns
creaking boats waiting for
captains who will never return

funeral bells
    snow
        descending
ashes of moonlight
on the pines

ABOUT THE AUTHOR

JIM BAINBRIDGE is a graduate of Harvard Law School and a National Science Foundation Fellowship recipient for graduate studies at UC Berkeley, from which he received a PhD Candidate Degree in mathematics. He has received numerous awards for his poetry and short stories, which have appeared in more than 50 literary journals in the USA, UK, Canada, Australia, Japan, and the Netherlands.

www.ingramcontent.com/pod-product-compliance
Lightning Source LLC
Chambersburg PA
CBHW031607040426
42452CB00006B/434